LIFE CYCLES

River

Sean Callery

Consultant: David Burnie

KINGFISHER

First published 2012 by Kingfisher
an imprint of Macmillan Children's Books
a division of Macmillan Publishers Limited
20 New Wharf Road, London N1 9RR
Basingstoke and Oxford
Associated companies throughout the world
www.panmacmillan.com

ISBN 978-0-7534-3340-9

1 3 5 7 9 8 6 4 2
1TR/1211/WKT/UNTD/140MA

A CIP catalogue record for this book is available from the British Library.

Printed in China

Note to readers: the website addresses listed in this book are correct at
the time of going to print. However, due to the ever-changing nature
of the internet, website addresses and content can change. Websites
can contain links that are unsuitable for children. The publisher cannot
be held responsible for changes in website addresses or content, or for
information obtained through a third party. We strongly advise that
internet searches be supervised by an adult.

The publisher would like to thank the following for permission to reproduce their material. Every care has been taken to trace copyright holders. However, if there
have been unintentional omissions or failure to trace copyright holders, we apologize and will, if informed, endeavour to make corrections in any future edition.

Top = t; Bottom = b; Centre = c; Left = l; Right = r

All artwork Stuart Jackson-Carter (Peter Kavanagh Art Agency)

Cover c Getty/NGS; cover tl Alamy/BE Eyley; cover tcl Naturepl/Colin Seddon; cover tcr Shutterstock/S Cooper Digital; cover tr Shutterstock/SJ Watt; back cover t Shutterstock/
alslutsky; back cover c Shutterstock/Cosmin Manci; back cover b Shutterstock/Tatiana53; page 1 Shutterstock/Brian Lasenby; 2 Shutterstock/Hintau Aliaksei; 3t Shutterstock/
Gert Ellstrom; 3b Shutterstock/thieury; 4tr Shutterstock/Gary Unwin; 4bl Alamy/Leo Kanaka; 4br Shutterstock/Bluerain; 4–5c Murray Robbins; 5tl Shutterstock/Image Focus; 5cr
Shutterstock/Soyka; 5bc Shutterstock/Paul Cowan; 5br Shutterstock/contax66; 6bl Naturepl/Jane Burton; 6tr Travis Tuten/Florida Wildlife Conservation; 7tl Shutterstock/Corneliu
LEU; 7tr Shutterstock/Jakez; 7ct Shutterstock/Corneliu LEU; 7c Photoshot/Nigel Downer; 7cb Canstock; 7br Shutterstock/Tatiana53; 7br Shutterstock/Gualberto Becerra; 7br
Shutterstock/Jakez; 8bl Naturepl/Gerrit Vyn; 8tr Alamy/David Hosking; 8br Photolibrary/OSF; 9tl Getty/Panoramic Images; 9tr Shutterstock/CLM; 9ct Shutterstock/Mariusz S
Jurgielewicz; 9c Shutterstock/John A Anderson; 9b Naturepl/Gerrit Vyn; 9br Shutterstock/Paul Cowan; 9br Shutterstock/Nikita Tiunov; 9br Thesupermat/Wikipedia; 9br Shutterstock/
Vladimir Daragan; 10bl Biopix; 11tr Shutterstock/camellia; 11ct Shutterstock/SimonG; 11c Shutterstock/Bill Kennedy; 11cb Photoshot/NHPA; 11cb Photoshot/NHPA; 11br
Shutterstock/Lim Yong Hian; 11br Shutterstock/Susan Montgomery; 12bl Frank Lane Picture Agency (FLPA)/Kevin Schafer/Minden; 13tl Naturepl/Kevin Schafer; 13tr Alamy/Prisma;
13ct Gregory Ochocki; 13cb Photolibrary/Bios; 13br Shutterstock/Eduardo Rivero; 13br Shutterstock/guentermanaus; 14l Naturepl/Andy Sands; 14br Photolibrary/OSF; 15tl Alamy/
Martin Fowler; 15tr Shutterstock/cami; 15ct Photolibrary/OSF; 15c Shutterstock/Mr Green; 15cb Shutterstock/Milena; 15bl Alamy/Wildlife GmbH; 15br Shutterstock/Dave Green;
15br Photolibrary/Bios; 16l Alamy/Peter Arnold Inc; 16tr Alamy/blickwinkel; 16br Alamy/blickwinkel; 17tl Photolibrary/Bios; 17tr Shutterstock/Blacqbook; 17ct Shutterstock/Ingrid
Prats; 17c Getty/NGS; 17bc Photolibrary/Bios; 17bl Corbis/Visuals Unlimited; 17br Shutterstock/Vasiliy Koval; 17br Shutterstock/Antoni Murcia; 18l Naturepl/Eric Baccega; 18tr
Science Photo Library/Leonard Lee Rue III/Leonard Rue Enterprises; 18br FLPA/Yva Momatiuk & John Eastcott; 19tl Shutterstock/oksana.perkins; 19tr Shutterstock/Soyka; 19ct
Shutterstock/Laura Duellman; 19c Shutterstock/Lukich; 19bc Shutterstock/Dennis Donohue; 19bl Naturepl/Eric Baccega; 19br Shutterstock/Sally Scott; 19br Shutterstock/
oksana.perkins; 19br Shutterstock/Steve McWilliam; 20l Naturepl/Simon Colmer; 20tr Shutterstock/Eric Etman; 20br FLPA/Jurgen & Christine Sohns;
21tc Shutterstock/ Darkpurple; 21tr Shutterstock/Kuttelvaserova; 21ct Shutterstock/Eric Etman; 21c Shutterstock/Sinelyov; 21bc Photolibrary/Imagebroker; 21bl FLPA/Foto Natura
Stock; 21br Shutterstock/Stuart Monk; 21br Shutterstock/Cosmin Manci; 21br Shutterstock/Videowokart; 22l FLPA/Rene Krekels; 22tr Photolibrary/Peter Arnold Inc; 22br FLPA/
Rene Krekels; 23tl Naturepl/Stephen Dalton; 23tr Shutterstock/Yanfei Sun; 23tc Naturepl/Màrk Yates; 23c FLPA/Thomas Marent/Minden; 23bc Shutterstock/WitR; 23bl FLPA/
Rene Krekels; 23br Shutterstock/Pavel Mikoska; 23br Shutterstock/phdwhite; 24l Naturepl/Andrew Parkinson; 24tr FLPA/Michael Callan; 24br Photolibrary/Bios; 25tl Naturepl/
Kim Taylor; 25tr Shutterstock/Elenamiv; 25tc Getty/Dave King/DK Images; 25c Photolibrary/Ludwig Werle/Picture Press; 25bc Photolibrary/Ludwig Werle/Picture Press; 25bl FLPA/
Dickie Duckett; 25br Shutterstock/slowfish; 25br Shutterstock/S Cooper Digital; 25br Shutterstock/vaklav; 26l FLPA/Paul Hobson/Holt; 26tr Photoshot/NHPA; 26br Naturepl/Colin
Seddon; 27tl FLPA/Imagebroker; 27tr Shutterstock/olinchuk; 27ct Shutterstock/Steve Byland; 27c Shutterstock/S Cooper Digital; 27bc Shutterstock/Reinhold Leitner; 27bl Alamy/
Lee Dalton; 27br Shutterstock/photocami; 27br Shutterstock/Graeme Dawes; 27br Shutterstock/S Cooper Digital; 27br Shutterstock/MarkMirror; 30tl Shutterstock/Ken Tan; 30bl
Shutterstock/alslutsky; 31tr Shutterstock/hfuchs; 31br Shutterstock/alsutsky; 32tl Shutterstock/Vitaly Titov; 32tr Shutterstock/Cosmin Manci

Contents

Introduction 4

Rivers of South America
Catfish 6
Cormorant 8
Piranha 10
River dolphin 12

Rivers of North America
Mayfly 14
Brook trout 16
Grizzly bear 18

Ponds of Europe
Great pond snail 20
Great crested newt 22
Little grebe 24
Otter 26

A European pond food web 28
Glossary and weblinks 30
Index 32

Introduction

Rivers and ponds are freshwater habitats for many plants and animals. Rivers carry water from hills and mountains down to seas or lakes. Ponds are home to animals that need to live in still water.

Some animals live in the water, others at the water's edge, and some come to drink. They must all eat to live. The list of who eats who is called a food chain.

Next, there are plant-eating animals, such as beavers that eat tree bark, twigs and leaves. These creatures are called consumers because they eat other living things.

Plants, such as reeds and water lilies, moss and algae, make their own food using energy from the sun. They are called producers and are first in a food chain.

Then there are more consumers, which catch and eat animals and insects. A kingfisher is one of these. It lives beside rivers, hunting and eating fish.

This book takes you along two river food chains and one pond food chain in different parts of the world. You will learn about the life cycles of 11 animals: how they are born, grow, reproduce and die.

At the top of a food chain is a predator that is so big, strong and fast that no other animal can catch it. This spot-billed pelican, which mainly eats fish, is a top predator.

Catfish

Sailfin catfish live in the rivers of the Amazon basin in South America. They scrape algae from logs and rocks with their large sucker mouths. They also eat plants.

1 The male fish digs a deep burrow in the riverbank below the water's surface. This will be a nesting tunnel.

2 The female lays thousands of eggs about a metre inside the tunnel. The male fertilizes and then guards them. He keeps the eggs healthy by moving the water around them.

Did you know?

Catfish are named after the whiskers, called barbels, on their heads. They help the fish to find food.

Sailfin catfish use their sucker mouths to pull algae from rocks and other surfaces.

Spines make the fins on their backs stand up. This makes the fish more difficult to swallow and puts off predators.

4 In another five days, they leave the burrow. They use their sucker mouths to grip surfaces, mostly resting by day and looking for food at night.

3 In ten days, the eggs hatch into larvae. These tiny see-through fish stay in the burrow, protected by their father and fed by yolk sacs attached to their bodies.

Sailfin catfish can live for 15 years if they reach adulthood. They have many predators, not all of them fish...

Cormorant

Cormorants dive and swim under the water to grab their prey. Sometimes they hunt together, beating the water with their wings to drive fish into the shallows where they are easier to catch.

1 Cormorants mate for life. Both parents make a nest of sticks and grass in a tree. The female lays up to five eggs.

2 The parents take turns to keep the eggs warm for 25–30 days. Then the chicks hatch out of their shells. They are born without any feathers.

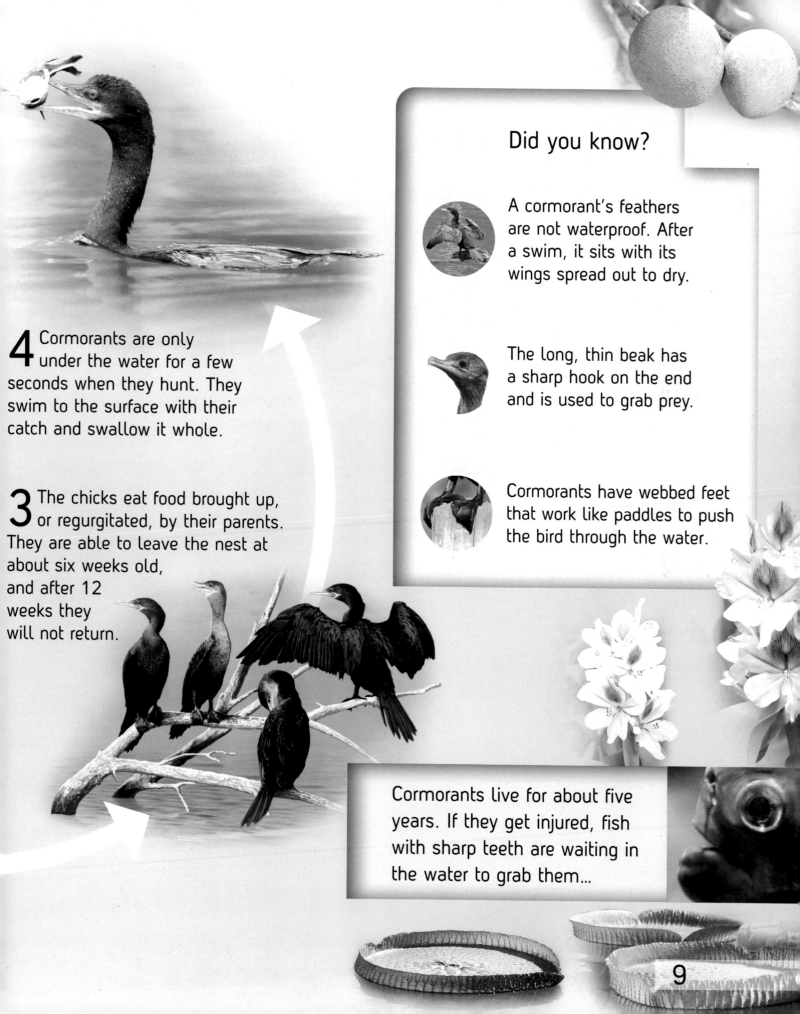

Did you know?

A cormorant's feathers are not waterproof. After a swim, it sits with its wings spread out to dry.

The long, thin beak has a sharp hook on the end and is used to grab prey.

Cormorants have webbed feet that work like paddles to push the bird through the water.

4 Cormorants are only under the water for a few seconds when they hunt. They swim to the surface with their catch and swallow it whole.

3 The chicks eat food brought up, or regurgitated, by their parents. They are able to leave the nest at about six weeks old, and after 12 weeks they will not return.

Cormorants live for about five years. If they get injured, fish with sharp teeth are waiting in the water to grab them...

Piranha

When a shoal of red-bellied piranhas attacks, thousands of sharp teeth strip the flesh from the prey in seconds. These fish eat any meat and will sometimes attack young or injured birds.

1 The male piranha makes a bowl-shaped nest with its tail and swims in circles over it to attract a female. She lays about 5,000 eggs, he fertilizes them, and both fish guard them.

2 After a few days, the eggs hatch into tiny fish. They hide among the plants, feeding on the yolk sacs attached to their bodies.

Did you know?

Piranha teeth are razor-sharp to slice flesh off their prey. If one tooth breaks, a new one grows in its place.

The large, powerful tail pushes the fish's narrow, streamlined body fast through the water.

Smell is more useful than sight for fish hunting in muddy waters. Piranhas also have sensors along their bodies to pick up the movement of prey.

4 The toughest fish in the shoal lead an attack. Other piranhas sense the splashing, blood and noise and join in, so large prey is eaten up quickly.

3 Young piranhas often take small bites out of the fins of other fish in the shoal for an easy little meal. This is called fin nipping.

Piranhas can live for five years, but they are not the only hunters in the water...

River dolphin

The river dolphin glides through the dark, muddy river water. It sends out clicking sound signals that hit prey, such as piranhas, and then bounce back. This tells the dolphin exactly where the prey is. Then it attacks.

1 River dolphins mate every 4–5 years. A single baby, known as a calf, grows inside the female for 9–12 months.

2 The dolphin calf is born between May and July when the river water is highest and there is lots of food.

A river dolphin has 140 blunt teeth. The ones at the front grab and crush prey while the back teeth grind it up.

It has a very bendy body and neck so it can twist easily between tree roots and search for food in hollow logs.

Dolphins breathe air through a blowhole on the head. The blowhole closes when the dolphin dives.

4 Adult dolphins may be white, pink, yellow, brown, grey or black. They are always on the move, swimming up to 30 kilometres in a day.

3 The calf suckles milk from its mother for at least a year. After that, it eats solid food, such as fish and crabs. Parent and calf stay together for two-and-a-half years.

River dolphins can live for 30 years. They have no predators, so they are at the top of many food chains.

Mayfly

Dark olive mayflies feed on algae in the streams and rivers of North America. They are sometimes called 'one-day flies' because they only live as adults for a few hours.

1 Females lay thousands of eggs on the surface of the water. The eggs quickly sink and settle on plants and rocks on the riverbed.

2 After a few days, each egg hatches into a nymph. It swims to find food and moults many times as it grows.

4 Adults fly up into the air in their thousands to find mates. They do not have proper mouthparts so they cannot eat. Once they have mated, they fall into the water and die.

3 After a few months, the nymph, now called a dun, rises to the water's surface. It has wings, but it cannot fly. It moults once more to get stronger adult wings for flying.

Did you know?

Mayfly nymphs grow gills, which they use to breathe under the water.

A male mayfly has large eyes shaped like turrets. They help it to find a mate quickly.

Mayflies hold their wings upright, just like butterflies. The wings are see-through and very fragile.

The huge numbers of mayfly nymphs, duns and adults make an easy meal for many other river creatures...

Brook trout

Brook trout live in cold streams and rivers, and feast on mayflies. They are born in shallow streams, migrate to deeper waters and then return as adults to breed.

1 In autumn, the female uses her tail to make a nest on the stream bed. Then she lays up to 600 eggs and the male fertilizes them.

2 Within 100 days, the eggs hatch into tiny fish called alevin. They stay safe in the nest, feeding on the yolk sacs attached to their bodies.

4 Adult fish swim far downriver to deeper waters. After two years, they are ready to breed, or spawn, and they return to the shallow streams.

3 When they have eaten the yolk sac, the alevin swim to shallow water where there are fewer predators and lots of mayflies to eat.

Did you know?

Brook trout hunt mostly by sight, looking out for prey in the daytime or when the moon is bright.

Fish also use their ears to hear predators and prey, and special sensors in the skin along their sides that pick up vibrations in the water.

They have wide, flat tails that give them the power to swim upstream when it is time for them to spawn.

Brook trout live for up to five years, but they are easily spotted by predators when they swim upriver to spawn...

Grizzly bear

Grizzly bears are furry giants that mostly eat plants. However, sharp claws and strong teeth allow them to feast on meat and fish when they can find it, including trout and salmon.

1 After mating, the female finds a den where she hibernates for the winter. Here, she gives birth to two cubs. They are toothless and almost hairless.

2 The cubs' eyes open after six weeks. They feed on their mother's rich, fatty milk while she snoozes.

Long, curved front claws and strong legs are perfect tools for digging up plants and roots as well as grabbing fish.

A grizzly's large snout gives it a strong sense of smell that it uses to find food and to get to know its territory.

A grizzly's 42 teeth are not sharp but they are perfect for chewing nuts, berries and plants, and gnawing meat.

4 Adult grizzlies mostly live alone, although they sometimes come together to catch fish migrating upstream. They can breed from the age of five.

3 In the spring, the cubs follow their mother away from the den. They will stay with her for about two years.

Grizzlies are most likely to die fighting each other. They are a top predator and can live for 30 years.

Great pond snail

Great pond snails live in ponds and slow-moving rivers across Europe. They stay near the water's surface, eating pond weed and scraping algae from rocks with their rough tongues.

1 Snails have male and female parts, so they can take it in turns to mate with each other. Both will then produce eggs.

2 They lay about 100 eggs on weeds and other plants. The eggs are held together in a special jelly, but many are still washed away or eaten by predators.

4 A pond snail has a lung for breathing air, but it can also breathe through its skin so it can stay underwater for months.

3 Baby snails are born after about four weeks. Each baby eats the remains of its egg, which helps it to grow a shell to protect its soft body.

Did you know?

As a snail grows, its shell gets lines on it. You can tell an old snail because it will have lots of lines on its shell.

The great pond snail eats grains of sand to help it break down tough plants that are difficult to digest.

Pond snails have tentacles with simple eyes at the end that help them to tell light from dark.

A pond snail can live for five years, but some animals love to eat its juicy body and even its crunchy shell...

Great crested newt

Newts look like lizards but they are really more like frogs with tails. They are amphibians, able to live both on land and in water. Newts eat tadpoles and young frogs, snails and insects.

1 Great crested newts mate in spring. The female lays 2–3 eggs a day on underwater plants, up to a total of 250. She folds each one in a leaf to protect it.

2 It takes three weeks for a tadpole to form inside the egg. Then it hatches and feeds on algae and small animals, including other tadpoles.

Did you know?

Newts shed their skin all their lives. They sometimes eat the old skin when they have moulted.

In the breeding season, males grow a tall, wavy crest along the spine and tail. This shows that they are ready to mate.

Newts use their tails as paddles to help them swim fast through the water.

4 Adult newts live on land but close to water, and they hibernate through the winter. They return to their birth pond to breed after three years.

3 The young newt has frilly gills so that it can breathe in the water. When it moults, the gills are replaced with lungs so it can live on land and breathe air.

Newts can live for ten years or longer if they escape the many dangers above and under the water...

Little grebe

The little grebe is happiest when it is in water. This bird is clumsy on land but moves gracefully when it dives to catch prey, such as newts and fish.

1 After mating, both parents build a floating nest where the female lays up to five eggs. They hide the eggs under weeds if they have to leave the nest.

2 The chicks hatch and the parents feed them tadpoles and small insects. Later, they take the chicks out on the water, dropping prey for them to chase.

Little grebes have large feet with wide toes. They do not walk well on land as their legs are far back on their bodies and they find it difficult to balance.

A grebe can press its thick feathers close to its body or puff them up to change how high it floats in the water.

A long, pointed beak is perfect for snapping up and holding on to wriggling fish and newts.

4 Adult grebes are excellent swimmers. They can stay under the water for almost a minute, travelling up to 30 metres as they search for food.

3 The chicks often ride on their parents' backs. Sometimes an adult even dives underwater with a chick still sitting there!

Little grebes can live for more than six years, but fast-moving predators can catch and eat young ones...

Otter

Otters look cute but they are deadly. Lightning-fast on land and in water, they chase down prey, such as fish and young or injured birds, and snap them up with their sharp teeth.

1 After mating, the female builds a shelter, called a holt, on the riverbank. It always has a tunnel underneath it so she can slip straight into the water unseen.

2 About two months later, she produces a litter of up to four cubs. Blind at first, they open their eyes within a month and soon learn to swim.

4 After a year, young otters leave their mother to find their own territory. They can breed when they are three years old.

3 Otter cubs suckle milk from their mother for four months. They learn to hunt by watching her and playing games with each other.

Did you know?

An otter's webbed paws work like flippers to help it swim fast and turn quickly in the water.

Its body is covered with tough hairs coated in oil. Its skin never gets wet, however long it spends in the water.

Whiskers help otters to feel vibrations. Even when the water is muddy, they can find prey without getting tangled up in weeds.

Otters only live for three or four years. They have no natural predators, but pollution in the water can kill them.

A European pond food web

This book follows two river food chains and one pond food chain. Most animals eat more than one food so they are part of many food chains. There are lots of food chains in rivers and ponds, and they link up like a map to make a food web.

Grey heron

Minnow

Otter

Little grebe

Water mite

Frog

Zooplankton

Sun

Newt

Snail

Algae

Glossary

ALGAE
Plant-like living things that make their food using the sun's energy.

AMAZON RIVER BASIN
Part of South America where the Amazon and other rivers flow together.

BURROW
A hole or tunnel in the ground used as a shelter by an animal.

CONSUMER
A living thing that survives by eating other living things.

FERTILIZE
When sperm from a male animal joins with the egg of a female to make a new life.

FRAGILE
Something that is easy to break.

GILLS
What fish and newts use to breathe under water.

HABITAT
The natural home of an animal.

HIBERNATE
To rest through the winter.

LARVA
A young insect that will change its body shape to become an adult. Groups are called larvae.

LITTER
A group of baby animals born to the same mother.

MATE
When a male and female animal reproduce. For some animals, this happens at a special time of year, called the mating season. Another word for mating is breeding.

MIGRATE
To go on a journey to a new habitat.

MOULT
When an animal gets rid of the outside of its body. This is also called shedding.

NYMPH
A young insect that is not yet fully grown and has no wings.

PREDATOR
An animal that kills and eats other animals.

PREY
An animal hunted by a predator.

PRODUCER
A living thing that makes its own food.

SAC
A bag of food attached to a baby animal.

SHOAL
A large group of fish.

SPAWN
When fish release their eggs to be fertilized.

SPINE
Part of an animal that sticks out from its body and is shaped like a needle.

STREAMLINED
When an animal is narrow and smooth to help it move easily through water.

SUCKER MOUTH
Some fish have this type of mouth to help them suck algae from the surface of rocks.

SUCKLE
When a young animal drinks milk from its mother's body.

TADPOLE
The form of a frog before it is adult.

TENTACLE
Part of a snail's body, used to feed and feel.

TERRITORY
The area where an animal hunts and keeps out rivals.

WEBBED
When toes are joined together with thin skin.

YOLK
The goodness inside an egg that feeds a new baby animal.

These websites have information about rivers and ponds, or their animals, or both!

- bbc.co.uk/cbbc/wild/amazinganimals
- ehow.co.uk/facts_5294605_common-newt-life-cycle.html
- kiddyhouse.com/Snails/snail.html#pondsnails
- kids.nationalgeographic.com/kids/animals/?source NavKidsAnimal
- nationalzoo.si.edu/audiences/kids
- thekidsgarden.co.uk/how-create-frog-friendly-pond.html
- wildengland.com
- zoobooks.com/virtualzoo.aspx?n=676484

Index

A
algae 4, 6,14, 20, 22, 29
Amazon river 6–13
America, North 14–19
amphibians 22

B
beaks 9, 25
bears, grizzly 18–19
beavers 4
birds 5, 8–9, 10, 24–25,
  26, 28
blowholes 13
burrows 6, 7

C
calves 12, 13
catfish 6–7
chicks 8, 9, 24, 25
claws 18, 19
consumers 4, 5
cormorants 8–9
cubs 18, 19, 26, 27

D
dens 18, 19
dolphins, river 12–13

E
eggs 6, 8, 10, 14, 16, 20,
  21, 22, 24
Europe 20–29
eyes 15, 18, 21, 26

F
feathers 8, 9, 25
feet 9, 25
fish 5, 6–7, 8, 10–11, 13,
  16–17, 18, 19, 24, 26, 28

food chains 4, 5, 13, 28
food webs 28–29
frogs 22, 29

G
gills 15, 23
grebes, little 24–25, 28

H
herons 28
hibernating 18, 23
hunting 8, 9, 17, 27

I
insects 5, 14–15, 22, 29

K
kingfishers 5

L
larvae 7
lungs 21, 22

M
mating 8, 12, 15, 17, 18,
  19, 20, 22, 23, 24, 26, 27
mayflies 14–15, 16, 17
meat 10, 18, 19
milk 13, 18, 27
minnows 28
moulting (shedding) 14, 23

N
nests 6, 8, 10, 16, 24
newts, great crested 22–23,
  24, 25, 29
nymphs 14, 15

O
otters 26–27, 28

P
pelicans 5
piranhas 10–11, 12
plants 4, 18, 19, 22
predators 5, 7, 11, 17, 19,
  20, 25, 27
prey 8, 9, 10, 11, 12, 13,
  17, 24, 26, 27
producers 4

S
sensors 11, 17
smell 11, 19
snails, great pond 20–21,
  22, 29
sun 4, 29
swimming 8, 13, 14, 17, 23
  25, 26

T
tadpoles 22
tails 10, 11, 16, 17, 23
teeth 10, 11, 13, 18, 19, 26
trout, brook 16–17, 18

W
water mites 29
wings 8, 9, 15

Y
yolk sacs 7, 10, 16

Z
zooplankton 29